by Joy Klein
illustrated by Rex Barron

## Harcourt
SCHOOL PUBLISHERS

Printed in China

ISBN 10: 0-15-350686-5
ISBN 13: 978-0-15-350686-4

Ordering Options
ISBN 10: 0-15-350600-8 (Grade 3 On-Level Collection)
ISBN 13: 978-0-15-350600-0 (Grade 3 On-Level Collection)
ISBN 10: 0-15-357907-2 (package of 5)
ISBN 13: 978-0-15-357907-3 (package of 5)

11 12 13 14 15 0940 12 11 10

I am still the king, I think. I have been ruler of this house for as long as I can remember. I did not inherit my kingdom. Mr. and Mrs. Smith and their daughter, Emma, brought me here to rule as a puppy. I have done as well as I could. I have barked at the mail carrier. I have kept the ridiculous squirrels from the yard. I have taken the Smiths for their walks. I have played with them so they get their exercise. I have made sure that no scraps of food remain on the floors.

My subjects have treated me royally in return. They feed me on schedule. They give me treats when I insist on having them. They brush my royal coat to its full beauty. I sleep when and where I choose. True, there is the noisy bird that talks all day and the silly hamster that runs all night. Don't be fooled, though. They are also my subjects. One good woof quiets them right down.

Now everything has changed! I can no longer
relax in the sunshine. I cannot even take a decent
rest now. My humans are not my faithful servants
anymore. They even turn their backs on me at times.
I cannot believe this has happened. I did not see it
coming. I was not prepared.

It began on a June morning. The humans, having done their duty in preparing my food, got into the large rolling thing. I watched them get in it, and then I settled down for a nice nap. They did not go anywhere, though. They came back right away, carrying some misshapen scruff of a thing.

"Poor little kitty," Emma said. "It must have been so frightened when it was trapped up inside the car's motor."

"It's a good thing we heard it before I started the car," said Father.

"Let me see if I can clean the poor thing up," said Mother. "She's so sweet."

I was curious, of course, so I tried to sniff at the thing, but they blocked me from it. "No Arthur," said Emma. "Get back, boy."

I could hardly believe what happened next. Father put me on the back porch. Nothing could have prepared me for it. At first, I thought he was taking me out to play fetch, which he loves. As soon as I went through the door, though, he closed it behind me! I had been barred from the kitchen, which is the center of my kingdom!

My emotion was simple shock at first. I did
not panic, though. I realized that the thing was a
young cat. I knew about cats. I had no fondness for
them, but they were not a problem. No cat dared
to invade my yard. As I thought about it, I rather
admired my people. They had saved the cat and
were caring for it. It seemed a nice bit of kindness
before they sent it on its way.

The cat did not go on its way the next day, though. Nor did it leave the next day or the next. In the meantime, I ruled only the porch. On the fourth day, I came back to my kitchen.

"Here, Arthur," Emma said. "Meet Summer. Isn't that a pretty name for a cat?"

I came closer, and the disgraceful thing scratched my tender nose. "Yow!" I barked.

"Whoa," Father said, grabbing my collar. "I guess you're not ready yet."

When it became clear that the cat would stay, I gently explained to her who was in charge. "Harrumph," Summer said as she walked along the countertop. Then she left the room.

A long struggle began. She went where she pleased. She went in things, on things, and over things. I could not control her. *She* warmed the humans' laps at night. They petted *her* while watching the loud picture box.

As the cat grew, she became bolder. Sometimes she teased me. She was quick, and I could not catch her. She would run under something and meow loudly. Then someone would come and put me on the porch.

At first, Hamster thought my troubles were funny. "Hey, King Arthur," he said. "Who's the boss now?" When Hamster awoke one evening to find Summer on top of his cage staring down at him, he did not think it was so funny anymore.

Bird was always on my side. "Trouble, trouble!"
she squawked whenever she saw Summer. The cat
just looked at her with a smile.

That cat was not stupid. When the family went
out, she disappeared. I never knew where she went.
"I just do whatever I please," she told me one day.

"If you don't bother me, I won't bother you,"
I said.

"Bother you?" she said. "I hardly think about
you at all."

The cat and I have reached an uneasy truce. She is part of the family now, but I don't know why. She doesn't take the Smiths for walks. She doesn't care about the noisy mail carrier. She sleeps on furniture. Neither Hamster nor Bird trust her, but the humans like her a lot. She pretends to like them, too, rubbing their ankles and making strange noises from her throat. I sleep lightly because I feel it is my duty to keep an eye on her.

I am still the king. I think.

# Think Critically

**1.** Why does Arthur regard himself as a king?

**2.** How would you describe Arthur?

**3.** What is Arthur's view of his kingdom at the end of the story?

**4.** Why does the author have Arthur call a car a "large rolling thing" and a television a "loud picture box"?

**5.** What part of the story did you think was the funniest? Why?

 **Social Studies**

**Kings and Queens** Arthur thinks of himself as the leader of his kingdom. Some countries have kings and queens. They are called "monarchies." Look up some countries that have kings or queens. Make a list of the countries. Find them on a map.

**School-Home Connection** Some people like cats. Some people like dogs. Some people like both. Ask friends and family members if they had to choose one or the other, which they would choose. Ask as many people as you can, and keep track of the results of your poll. Share your results with the class.

**Word Count:** 897

GRADE 3

Lesson 23

WORD COUNT

897

GENRE

Fantasy

LEVEL

See TG or go Online

GO online Harcourt Leveled
Readers Online Database

ISBN-13: 978-0-15-350686-4
ISBN-10: 0-15-350686-5

9 780153 506864

90000>

Harcourt
SCHOOL PUBLISHERS

# Groundhog's New Home

by Keith Yoder

illustrated by
Wallace Keller

Ben K.